FANTASY WRITING 101

All Your Questions Answered

HACKNEY AND JONES

Copyright © 2023 by Hackney and Jones

All rights reserved.

No part of this book may be reproduced in any form or by any electronic or mechanical means, including information storage and retrieval systems, without written permission from the author, except for the use of brief quotations in a book review.

Contents

Foreword	v
Introduction	vii
1. How Do Fantasy Writers Make Money?	1
2. Quick Tips For Fantasy Writers Starting Out	3
3. Popular Fantasy Novels	8
4. Common Fears When Writing A Novel	10
5. Fears About Writing A Fantasy	12
6. Fantasy Writing Mistakes To Avoid	18
7. Fantasy Writing Checklist	21
8. Plotting Or Pantsing?	24
9. Point Of View In Novel Writing	27
10. Coming Up With An Idea For Your Fantasy Novel	31
11. Some Fantasy Writing Prompts For You	35
12. Plotting And Structuring Your Novel	38
13. Creating A Compelling Opening Scene	42
14. Creating Characters	45
15. How To Incorporate Emotions Into Your Fantasy Novel	54
16. Plot Twists	58
17. Red Herrings	63
18. Using Descriptive Language	66
19. Writing Dialogue In Your Fantasy Novel	69
20. How To End Your Novel	74
21. Fantasy Novel Book Titles	81
22. Fantasy Writing Word Count	83
23. Fantasy Fiction Book Cover Tips	85
24. Editors And Proofreaders	88
25. Book Marketing	90
26. Fantasy Writing Glossary	96
Now what…?	99

Foreword

We are Claire and Vicky from **Hackney and Jones Publishing**. Together, we have created, written, and published hundreds of fiction and non-fiction books and have learned a fair bit along the exciting journey that is book publishing.

From our extensive experience in this field, we understand how difficult writing can be, whether it's fiction or non-fiction - which is why we're here to provide assistance.

Believe us, we've made our share of mistakes along the way. We've learned from them and now want to help you avoid them. That's why we've done all the research and hard work so you don't have to.

We know what it takes to craft an engaging book, and we want to share that expertise with you here.

But more than just experience, our passion is what drives us forward. Everyone has an important narrative to tell, so let us help you tell it in the best way possible.

Foreword

Writing can be a lonely pursuit, but it doesn't have to be. With our support, you'll have an objective guide and an encouraging friend at your side that will cheer you on as you reach success. Let us encourage and motivate you toward your objectives!

We believe in the power of stories to transform lives, to make us laugh or cry, and to inspire and challenge us - and we want to assist you with telling your own unique narrative.

We invite you to join us on this exciting journey. Whether you're an experienced writer or just starting out, our support and guidance can make the process smooth and turn your writing goals into reality.

Let's do this!

Introduction

Have you ever lost yourself in a book that takes you to a whole new world? A fantasy novel is just that - a story that unfolds in a world different from our own. This world may have magical creatures, dragons, or mystical elements that you won't find in reality.

To create a successful fantasy novel, there are a few key elements you'll want to include:

First up, world-building. This is where you create a unique and interesting world for your story to take place in. You'll need to think about geography, culture, history, and the magical systems that make this world special.

Craft characters that are engaging and relatable. The main characters, like heroes and villains, are crucial, but don't forget about the supporting characters - friends, family members, and mentors - who help bring the story to life.

A compelling plot is also a must. A fantasy novel often involves a quest or journey that the characters embark on to save the world

Introduction

or defeat a powerful enemy. There are endless possibilities, so get creative!

Magic is often a key feature in fantasy novels, so be sure to include it. This can take the form of spells, enchanted objects, or magical creatures that inhabit the world you've created.

Lastly, your story needs conflict to keep readers engaged. This can be physical, moral, or internal, but whatever it is, it should make your readers invested in the outcome.

By incorporating these key elements into your fantasy novel, you'll create a world readers will want to explore and characters they'll care about. So, let your imagination run wild and start crafting your own fantastical adventure!

How Do Fantasy Writers Make Money?

So, you're curious about how fantasy writers make a living? Let's break it down.

First up, book sales. When a fantasy writer creates a book, they can sell it to readers in many formats, whether that's a physical book you can pick up in a store or an e-book you can download onto your device. The writer typically gets a percentage of the sales, which can add up if the book becomes popular.

But that's not the only way to make money as a fantasy writer. If a book really takes off, it may catch the eye of movie or TV producers who want to adapt it for the screen. In this case, the writer can sell the rights to their story for a lot of money and may also receive a cut of the profits.

And let's not forget about merchandise! If a book becomes a sensation, fans might want to get their hands on all sorts of memorabilia, from t-shirts to action figures to posters. The writer can make money by licensing their characters and world to companies that make these items.

Finally, if a fantasy writer becomes famous enough, they might be invited to speak at events or schools, which can be another source of income.

Of course, making a living as a writer is no easy feat, and there's no guarantee of success. But if you have a passion for storytelling and keep honing your craft, you never know where it might take you. The key is to keep at it, keep writing, and keep dreaming big!

2

Quick Tips For Fantasy Writers Starting Out

If you're looking to write a killer fantasy novel, there are a few things you'll want to keep in mind.

Firstly, read a lot of fantasy books! This will give you a solid understanding of the genre and help you figure out what works and what doesn't in a fantasy story.

As you read, take notes on what you like and don't like about the books you're reading. This will help you develop your own style and avoid common pitfalls.

Don't just stick to your favourite sub-genre of fantasy - branch out and try reading books that take place in different worlds, have different magic systems, and feature different types of characters. This will help you expand your horizons and come up with fresh ideas.

Pay close attention to how authors structure their stories, reveal information, and build tension. This will help you develop your own writing skills.

When creating your own fantasy world, research is key. Take the time to research different aspects of your world, whether it's geography, history, culture, or magic. This will help you create a more realistic and immersive world.

Make sure that everything in your world fits together seamlessly. Consistency is vital, so avoid contradictions and plot holes.

Show, don't tell. Don't just dump information on your readers about your world - show them through your characters' actions and experiences.

If you're looking to write a great fantasy novel, creating memorable and relatable characters is a must.

Here are some tips to help you do just that:

Give your characters flaws. No one is perfect, so make sure your characters have flaws that make them more human and relatable.

Clear motivations are also important. Give your characters motivations that drive their actions and decisions throughout the story.

Diversity matters. Create characters with different backgrounds, personalities, and motivations to make your story more interesting and inclusive.

When planning your plot, there are a few things to keep in mind:

While some writers prefer to write by the seat of their pants, having a general idea of the plot and major story beats can help you stay focused and avoid writer's block.

Using an outline, even a rough one, can help you stay on track and avoid getting stuck.

Knowing your ending is crucial. It can help you write towards that ending and avoid unnecessary tangents.

As for ideas for endings, there are many possibilities! Here are just a few to consider:

- The hero defeats the evil villain and saves the world from destruction.
- The hero discovers a hidden power or magical artefact that helps them defeat the villain and restore peace to the land.
- The hero sacrifices themselves to save the world, but their actions inspire others to continue the fight.
- The hero realises that the true enemy was within themselves all along, and overcomes their inner demons to save the world.
- The hero and the villain team up to defeat a greater threat, but the villain ultimately sacrifices themselves for the greater good.
- The hero must make a difficult choice that determines the fate of the world, and they choose the selfless option that saves others at their own expense.

If you want to take your fantasy writing to the next level, developing subplots can add depth and complexity to your story. Consider how these subplots can intersect with the main plot and enhance your character's journeys.

One of the best ways to improve your writing is to practise every day. Set aside some time each day to write, even if it's just a few minutes. Make writing a part of your daily routine by setting a schedule.

If you're struggling for ideas, use writing prompts to get your creativity flowing. And don't be afraid to experiment with different styles, genres, and techniques during your daily writing time. This can help you find your voice as a writer.

Remember that your first draft is unlikely to be perfect, so don't be afraid to revise and edit until you're happy with the final product. And if you're looking for editing and proofreading services, our workbook, **"How To Write A Winning Fiction Book Outline - Fantasy Fiction Workbook,"** offers a 10% discount on both!

After you've finished your first draft, take a break from it for a few days or weeks. This will give you a fresh perspective when you come back to it. And when you're ready to revise, try reading your work aloud. This can help you catch errors and awkward phrasing you might miss when reading silently.

Fantasy Writing 101

Writing is a process, so be patient and enjoy the journey. With practice and dedication, you can create a fantasy novel that readers will love.

Receiving feedback is crucial to improving your writing, so share your work with others. Whether it's through a writing group, beta readers, or a professional editor, their critiques can help you identify areas that need improvement and elevate your story.

Joining a writing community is an excellent way to connect with other fantasy writers, exchange feedback, and share your writing journey. You can find many online communities where you can find writers with similar interests and participate in discussions.

For those who prefer face-to-face interactions, joining a local writing group or attending writing conferences and workshops can be a great opportunity to meet other writers, develop new skills, and receive feedback on your writing.

Remember that writing is not just about receiving feedback on your work, but also supporting others in their writing journey. Don't be afraid to read and critique the work of other writers in your community.

Above all, writing should be enjoyable and a channel to express your creativity. So take risks, experiment with different styles and techniques, and most importantly, have fun with the process!

3

Popular Fantasy Novels

The fantasy genre is one of the most popular among writers because of the sheer scope of themes and ideas it explores.

Here is a short selection of some popular fantasy novels:

"Harry Potter" series by J. K. Rowling: This beloved series follows the story of a young wizard, Harry Potter, as he attends Hogwarts School of Witchcraft and Wizardry and battles the dark wizard, Lord Voldemort. The books are popular for their engaging characters, intricate world-building, and relatable themes of friendship, courage, and standing up for what's right.

"The Lord of the Rings" trilogy by J. R. R. Tolkien: This classic trilogy follows a group of hobbits, elves, dwarves, and men as they journey across Middle Earth to destroy the One Ring and defeat the evil Lord Sauron. The books include detailed world-building, epic scope, and themes of good vs. evil, friendship, and the corrupting influence of power.

"The Chronicles of Narnia" series by C. S. Lewis: This

series follows a group of children as they travel to the magical world of Narnia, where they embark on adventures and help save the land from the White Witch and other foes. Popular for their imaginative world-building, these books include engaging characters and themes of faith, redemption, and self-discovery.

"Percy Jackson and the Olympians" series by Rick Riordan: This series follows a young demigod, Percy Jackson, as he discovers his true identity and goes on adventures with his friends to save the world of the Greek gods and monsters. The books have witty humour, engaging characters, and creative uses of mythology.

"Game of Thrones" series by George R. R. Martin: This epic fantasy series follows the political machinations and power struggles of various noble families in the land of Westeros, as they vie for the Iron Throne and face threats from beyond the Wall. These books include intricate world-building, complex characters, and themes of power, family, and loyalty.

All of these books offer immersive worlds, engaging characters, and exciting plots that capture readers' imaginations.

They also explore relatable themes and universal human experiences, making them appealing to a wide range of readers.

If your fantasy books include these elements, you will meet all the target market's requirements.

4

Common Fears When Writing A Novel

Writing a novel is a desire for many people. It even appears on many people's bucket lists, and it's widely said that "everyone has a book in them," whether that is a work of literary fiction or a memoir. But what is it that stops budding writers from writing a novel?

Fear of failure: Many writers are concerned that their novel may not be good enough or well-received by readers. To combat this fear, remind yourself that writing is a process and first drafts often require significant revisions. Focus on the enjoyment of writing and the accomplishment of completing a project, rather than stressing about the final outcome.

Fear of the blank page: Starting a new writing project can be daunting, particularly when confronted with an empty page or screen. To conquer this fear, break the project into smaller, manageable tasks. Set a goal to write a specific number of words daily, or create a rough outline to guide your writing.

Fear of the editing process: Writing the first draft is just the beginning, and many writers feel apprehensive about the subsequent revisions and editing. To alleviate this fear, approach the editing process with an open mind and a readiness to make changes. Recognise that editing offers the chance to refine the story and make it the best version possible.

Fear of rejection: After completing the novel, writers might be anxious about submitting it to agents or publishers and dealing with rejection. To address this fear, keep in mind that rejection is a normal aspect of the writing process. Don't take rejections personally; instead, use them as learning experiences to enhance your writing. And consider self-publishing, which can be a very lucrative option, as you will keep much more of the book royalty.

Fear of exposure: Writing a novel can be an intimate experience, and some writers might be uneasy about revealing their innermost thoughts and emotions to readers. To mitigate this fear, remember that writing is self-expression, and sharing your thoughts and feelings can create meaningful connections with readers. Start by sharing your work with trusted friends or family members, gradually building confidence in presenting it to a broader audience.

Fear of success: Although it may sound counterintuitive, some writers are apprehensive about the potential consequences of their novel's success. To conquer this fear, concentrate on the present moment and the pleasure of writing. Avoid worrying excessively about the future, and remember that success is a journey rather than a destination. Embrace the writing process and allow the future to unfold naturally.

5

Fears About Writing A Fantasy

If you're thinking about writing a fantasy story, it's normal to have some fears and worries about it.

Here are some common fears people have about writing fantasy fiction and why you shouldn't let them stop you from pursuing your dream:

"What if my story is not original enough?": Many fantasy stories share similar themes and tropes, but that doesn't mean your story won't be unique. Your characters, setting, and plot will all be your own, and your writer's voice will make your story distinct.

Some ideas for you:

Think outside the box: Challenge yourself to come up with ideas that are not commonly seen in fantasy stories. Look to other genres or real-life events for inspiration.

Use your personal experiences: Draw from your own experiences or emotions to infuse your story with authenticity and uniqueness.

Experiment with different writing styles: Try writing in a different style or tone than what you're used to. This can help you explore new ideas and find your voice as a writer.

Collaborate with others: Collaborate with other writers or artists to bring new perspectives and ideas to your story.

Embrace the familiar: Don't be afraid to use familiar fantasy tropes or themes, but put your own spin on them. Focus on creating compelling characters and unique settings that readers will connect with.

"What if I don't know enough about world-building?": World-building can seem daunting, but you don't need to be an expert to write a compelling fantasy story. Start with a basic outline of your world and add details as you go along. You can always conduct research or seek feedback from others to help fill in any gaps.

Some ideas for you:

Start with the basics: Begin with a basic outline of your world, including its geography, climate, history, and culture. This will provide a foundation for further details.

Develop a magic system: If your story involves magic, develop a consistent and logical system for how it works. Consider the limitations and consequences of using magic, as well as its history and cultural significance.

Add details as you go: As you write, add more details to your world-building. This can include specific locations, customs, and folklore. Don't worry about perfection on the first draft - you can always revise and add more details later.

Do research: Conduct research on topics relevant to your world-building, such as mythology, history, or cultural practices. This can help you create a more realistic and immersive world.

Seek feedback: Share your world-building with beta readers or writing groups to get feedback on consistency and believability. This can help you identify areas that need more work and ensure that your world makes sense to readers.

"What if my characters aren't interesting enough?": Characters are a key part of any story, but they don't have to be perfect or larger-than-life. Flawed and relatable characters can be just as compelling, if not more so. Focus on creating characters with distinct personalities and motivations that drive the plot forward.

Some ideas for you:

Give them a unique backstory: Develop a detailed backstory for each character, including their upbringing, experiences, and personality traits. This will help readers understand their motivations and actions throughout the story.

Eg. The character grew up in a small village plagued by a supernatural curse.

Give them flaws: No character is perfect, so give your characters flaws that make them relatable and human. This can include things like insecurities, bad habits, or moral ambiguities.

Eg. The character has a deep-seated fear of failure, which drives them to take unnecessary risks and make impulsive decisions.

Show, don't tell: Instead of telling readers about your characters' personalities, show their traits through their actions and dialogue. This can help readers connect with them on a deeper level.

Telling: *John was angry that he missed the bus.*
Showing: *John's face turned red, and he clenched his fists as he watched the bus drive away. "Why does this always happen to me?" he muttered under his breath.*

Create relationships: Develop relationships between your characters that are dynamic and complex. This can include romantic relationships, friendships, or even rivalries.

Use character questionnaires: Use character questionnaires to flesh out your characters' personalities, motivations, and backgrounds. This can help you create a more well-rounded and believable character.

Some ideas to help you write well-rounded, interesting characters:

- What is your character's name, age, and physical appearance?
- What is your character's occupation or role in the story?
- What is your character's backstory and how has it shaped them?
- What are your character's strengths and weaknesses?
- What are your character's goals and motivations?
- What are your character's fears and insecurities?
- What is your character's relationship with other characters in the story?
- What are your character's hobbies or interests outside of the main plot?
- What is your character's personality type (e.g. introverted, extroverted, etc.)?

- How does your character change or grow throughout the story?

"What if my story is too long or too short?": The length of your story will depend on the complexity of your plot and the depth of your world-building. Don't worry too much about length in the early stages of writing. Focus on telling the story you want to, and worry about trimming or expanding it later during the editing process.

Some ideas for you:

Use a three-act structure: A three-act structure can help you organise your story and ensure a clear beginning, middle, and end. This can help you avoid unnecessary tangents or plot holes.

Set a word count goal: Set a word count goal for your story based on your genre and the complexity of your plot. This can give you a benchmark to work towards and help you avoid overwriting or underwriting.

Outline your story: Use an outline to map out major plot points and beats. This can help you see where you may need to expand or trim certain scenes or chapters.

Seek feedback: Share your story with beta readers or writing groups to get feedback on pacing and length. Ask them if any parts of the story feel rushed or dragged out and use their feedback to adjust your pacing.

Cut unnecessary scenes: During the editing process, review your story for scenes or chapters that don't advance the plot or develop the characters. Cut these scenes to tighten your story and improve its pacing. *'Cut the fluff!'*

Fantasy Writing 101

"What if no one likes my story?": It's natural to want others to enjoy your writing, but not everyone will. Remember that writing is self-expression, and it's okay if not everyone connects with your work. Focus on writing the story you want to tell, and enjoy creating something new.

Some ideas for you:

Read reviews of bestselling fantasy fiction: Reading reviews of popular fantasy novels can give you insight into what readers enjoy and what to avoid. Use this knowledge to improve your own writing and avoid common pitfalls.

Develop a thick skin: Accept that not everyone will love your work, and that's okay. Don't take negative feedback personally, use it as an opportunity to grow and improve as a writer.

Celebrate your successes: Don't forget to celebrate your successes, no matter how small they seem. Finishing a draft, receiving positive feedback, or even just making progress on your writing goals are all accomplishments to be proud of.

Remember, writing a fantasy story should be a fun and creative process. Don't let your fears hold you back from exploring new worlds and characters, and don't be afraid to take risks and try new things.

6

Fantasy Writing Mistakes To Avoid

Novel writing can be extremely rewarding for an author, especially when they receive an excellent review. But it is all too easy to fall into the trap of bad habits in novel writing.

Here are the most common mistakes writers make and how to avoid them:

Info-dumping: Avoid dumping too much information about your world or characters in one go. This can overwhelm the reader and slow down the pacing of your story. Instead, reveal information gradually throughout the story and only include what's necessary to advance the plot.

Overused tropes: While familiar tropes and themes can comfort readers, overusing them can make your story feel clichéd and unoriginal.

Some examples:

- **The chosen one:** A hero destined to save the world and possesses unique powers or abilities.
- **The evil empire:** A powerful and oppressive empire or ruler that the protagonist must overthrow.
- **The mentor:** A wise and experienced character who guides the protagonist on their journey.
- **The magical artefact:** A magical object the protagonist must find or protect to save the world.
- **The love triangle:** A romantic subplot in which the protagonist must choose between two love interests.

To avoid falling into this trap, put your own spin on these tropes or create new ones altogether. Focus on creating unique characters, settings, and plot devices to make your story stand out.

Weak world-building: A poorly developed world can make your story feel flat and not engaging. To avoid this, focus on creating a well-crafted and believable world with a clear history, geography, culture, and magic system.

One-dimensional characters: Characters that are one-dimensional and lack depth can make your story feel flat and uninteresting. To avoid this, create characters with distinct personalities, motivations, and flaws. Use character questionnaires and other writing exercises to flesh out their backgrounds and make them feel like real people.

Lack of conflict: A story without conflict is a boring read. To avoid this, create obstacles and challenges for your characters to overcome. Use the three-act structure to map these out.

Poor pacing: A story that is too slow or fast-paced can be challenging for readers to engage with. To avoid this, use a combination of action, dialogue, and exposition to create a balanced pace that keeps readers engaged. Seek feedback from beta readers to help identify areas where the pacing may need adjustment.

7

Fantasy Writing Checklist

With any planning, having a checklist ensures you have included all the necessary elements.

Here is a comprehensive checklist for writing your fantasy novel:

Before writing:

- Identify your target audience and genre.
- Brainstorm your story idea and create a rough outline or synopsis.
- Research your world-building elements, such as magic systems or historical inspirations.
- Develop your main characters with unique personalities, motivations, and backgrounds.
- Set writing goals and establish a writing routine that works for you.

During writing:

- Use a three-act structure to guide your plot and pacing.
- Avoid info-dumping and reveal information gradually throughout the story.
- Focus on showing, not telling, through dialogue and action.
- Write in a consistent tone and point of view.
- Use sensory details to make your world and characters feel real and immersive.
- Write as frequently as possible to maintain momentum and consistency.

After writing:

- Take a break and let your story sit for a while before revising.
- Read through your story carefully and look for plot holes or inconsistencies.
- Cut unnecessary scenes or characters to tighten the pacing and focus on the main plot.
- Seek feedback from beta readers or writing groups to get constructive criticism.
- Revise and edit your story until you're happy with the final product.

Some additional tips to consider throughout the writing process:

- Avoid overusing fantasy tropes or clichés.
- Create a strong opening hook to draw readers in.
- Use conflict and obstacles to keep the story engaging and suspenseful.
- Ensure that your story has a clear resolution and satisfying ending.

- Celebrate your writing accomplishments, no matter how small they seem.

By following this checklist, you can ensure that your fantasy writing is well-developed, engaging, and consistent from start to finish.

8

Plotting Or Pantsing?

When writing a novel, there are two general approaches: **plotting** and **pantsing.**

Here are full explanations of each approach and its pros and cons.

Plotting

Plotting is a method of writing where the author creates a detailed outline or plan for the story before beginning to write. This can include a chapter-by-chapter outline, character sketches, and other notes to help guide the writing process.

Pros of plotting include:

- **Better organisation:** Plotting can help writers stay organised and on track with their story, making a coherent and well-structured novel.

- **Less writer's block:** Plotting can help reduce the chances of writer's block, as writers know where the story is headed and can focus on filling in the details.
- **More efficient:** Plotting can be a more efficient method of writing, as writers have a roadmap to follow and don't need to spend as much time figuring out where the story is going.

Cons of plotting include:

- **Limited flexibility:** Plotting can limit the flexibility of the writing process, as writers may feel constrained by the outline and have less room to explore new ideas.
- **Can feel too structured:** Some writers may find plotting too structured or formulaic, leading to a less creative or imaginative result.
- **Takes more time:** Plotting can take more time and effort upfront, as writers need to create a detailed outline before beginning to write.

Pantsing

Pantsing, also known as *"writing by the seat of your pants,"* is where the author starts with a general idea or concept and then allows the story to unfold as they write.

Pros of pantsing include:

- **More creativity:** Pantsing can lead to more creativity and spontaneity in the writing process, as writers explore new ideas and take the story in unexpected directions.
- **More flexibility:** Pantsing allows for more flexibility in the writing process, as writers can change direction or try new things without feeling constrained by an outline.

- **Faster writing:** Pantsing can be a faster method of writing, as writers can focus on getting the story down on paper without worrying about details or structure.

Cons of pantsing include:

- **More writer's block:** Pantsing can lead to more writer's block, as writers may not know where the story is going or how to move forward.
- **Can lead to less structure:** Pantsing can sometimes lead to a less structured or well-organised story, as writers may not have a clear sense of the overall plot or direction of the story.
- **More editing:** Pantsing can lead to more editing and revisions later as writers may need to go back and add structure or clarity to the story.

Ultimately, the choice between plotting and pantsing is personal, and different writers may find that one method works better for them than the other.

Some writers may even use a combination of both methods, starting with a rough outline and then allowing the story to evolve as they write. The most important thing is to find a way that works for you and helps you create the best possible novel.

9

Point Of View In Novel Writing

Point of view, or POV, is the perspective from which a story is told.

There are several different types of POV commonly used in novel writing, each with its own benefits and challenges.

Here is a detailed but easy-to-understand guide to POV in novel writing, along with tips and the benefits of each.

First-person POV

First-person POV is when the story is told from the main character's perspective, using "I" as the pronoun.

Benefits of first-person POV include:

- **Deep emotional connection:** First-person POV allows readers to get inside the head of the main

character, creating a deep emotional connection with them.
- **Intimate and personal:** First-person POV can create an intimate and personal feel to the story, as readers experience.
- **Greater control:** First-person POV can give the writer greater control over the narrative, as the reader only knows what the protagonist knows.

Tips for writing in first-person POV:

- **Stay consistent with the character's voice:** The protagonist's voice should be consistent throughout the story.
- **Avoid excessive self-reflection:** The protagonist should not spend too much time reflecting on themselves or their actions, as it can become repetitive.
- **Develop other characters:** Other characters must be developed as much as the protagonist is to create a well-rounded story.

Third-person limited POV

Third-person limited POV is when the story is told from the perspective of a single character, using "he" or "she" as the pronoun.

Benefits of third-person limited POV include:

- **Greater flexibility:** Third-person limited POV offers greater flexibility over the story and the narrative.
- **Ability to create multiple characters:** Third-person limited POV allows the writer to create multiple characters with unique perspectives and personalities.

- **Increased objectivity:** Third-person limited POV offers increased objectivity, as the writer can create distance between the reader and the protagonist.

Tips for writing in third-person limited POV:

- **Establish the main character early:** The main character should be established early to help the reader identify with them.
- **Avoid head-hopping:** You should avoid switching between different character perspectives within a scene.
- **Use vivid sensory details:** The writer should use vivid sensory details to help immerse the reader in the story.

Third-person omniscient POV

Third-person omniscient POV is when the story is told from the perspective of an all-knowing narrator, using "he" or "she" as the pronoun.

Benefits of third-person omniscient POV include:

- **Greater insight into the story:** Third-person omniscient POV allows the writer to give the reader greater insight into the story and its characters.
- **Increased flexibility:** Third-person omniscient POV offers increased flexibility, as the writer can move between characters and events as needed.
- **Ability to create suspense:** Third-person omniscient POV can create suspense, as the reader knows more than the characters.

Tips for writing in third-person omniscient POV:

- **Be careful with character knowledge:** Be mindful with what the narrator knows versus what the characters know to avoid plot holes.
- **Avoid head-hopping:** It's important to avoid head-hopping, which is when the writer switches between different character perspectives within a scene.
- **Use clear transitions:** The writer should use clear transitions when moving between different characters or events.

By understanding the different types of POV and their benefits and challenges, writers can choose the best approach for their story and create a compelling and engaging novel.

10

Coming Up With An Idea For Your Fantasy Novel

So, you've decided that now is the time for you to write your novel. But what if the will is there, but the idea is not? What do you do if you can't think of a single idea?

Here are some tips to help you pull that masterpiece out of your head:

Take inspiration from your own life: Draw on your own experiences with mystical occurrences for inspiration.

Combine different genres: Consider blending fantasy with other genres, such as sci-fi or mystery.

Take inspiration from real-life stories: Read real-life stories in the news or online and use them as inspiration for your fantasy novel.

Use writing prompts: Writing prompts can be a great way to generate ideas and spark creativity.

Explore different cultures: Explore different cultures and their traditions around fantasy and mysticism for inspiration.

Play with opposites: Consider pairing characters who are opposites in personality, background, or values.

Use music as inspiration: Listen to music that evokes a specific emotion or feeling and use it for your story.

Explore different time periods: Consider setting your story in a different time or era, such as the Victorian era or 1920s.

Use a dream journal: Keep a dream journal and use your dreams for your story.

Create a character first: Create a unique and compelling character and build the story around them.

Use setting as inspiration: Choose a unique or interesting setting, such as a small town or a remote island, and use it as inspiration for your story.

Use astrology as inspiration: Use astrology to create unique character traits.

Explore different sub-genres: Consider exploring different sub-genres of fantasy, such as fantasy romance or fantasy comedy.

Use mythology as inspiration: Draw on mythology or folklore for inspiration, such as the story of Cupid and Psyche.

Explore different age groups: Consider writing a fantasy novel that features characters from a different age group than your own.

Use different perspectives: Consider writing from the perspective of a non-human character.

Fantasy Writing 101

Read lots of fantasy books: One great way to get ideas for your own novel is to read fantasy books. This can help you understand what kinds of stories are already out there and what elements and themes are common in the genre. You can also note down what you like and don't like about different stories and use that to inform your own writing.

Brainstorm: Think about what kind of world you want to create, what kind of characters you want to include, and what story you want to tell. Write down as many ideas as possible, even if they seem silly or far-fetched.

Choose a focus: Once you have a lot of ideas, start to narrow them down and choose a focus for your novel. This could be a particular character, setting, or theme. Having a clear focus can help you stay on track as you write.

Create your world: If your fantasy novel is set in a different world or universe, take some time to create that world. Think about what the geography, history, and culture of that world might be like. You can draw maps, create timelines, and write histories to help you flesh out your world.

Develop your characters: Your characters are the heart of your story, so take time to develop them. Think about their personalities, motivations, and backstories. You can also draw sketches or create character sheets to help you visualise your characters.

Write an outline: Before writing your novel, write an outline to help you organise your ideas. This can include a summary of the plot, descriptions of each chapter, and notes on character development and world-building.

Don't forget: We fully recommend you invest in our accompanying workbook:

How To Write A Winning Fiction Book Outline - Fantasy Fiction Workbook

Start writing!: Once you have your outline, it's time to start writing! Don't worry too much about making it perfect at first; just focus on getting your ideas down on paper. You can always go back and revise later.

By using these methods, you can devise unique and interesting ideas for your fantasy novel that will captivate readers and keep them engaged from beginning to end.

11

Some Fantasy Writing Prompts For You

Here are some creative ideas to get your creative juices flowing:

1. In a world where magic is outlawed, a young apprentice must hide their powers while attempting to overthrow the corrupt government.
2. A cursed forest is home to a mysterious creature that grants wishes but at a terrible price. A group of adventurers enters the forest seeking their desires, but the cost of the creature's gifts is more than they imagined.
3. After discovering a hidden portal, a modern-day teenager finds themselves in a medieval world where they must use their knowledge of technology to survive and thrive.
4. A group of unlikely allies must band together to stop an ancient evil from taking over the world. However, each group member has a dark secret that could tear them apart.
5. A prince, cursed to live as a dragon, seeks out a powerful sorceress who can break the spell. He must battle other mythical creatures and confront his inner demons.

6. In a society where the ruling class has access to magical powers, a lower-class rebel must infiltrate the palace and steal a powerful artefact to even the playing field.
7. A young girl discovers she can communicate with animals and embarks on a quest to save a group of endangered creatures from a corrupt corporation.
8. In a world where time travel is possible, a group of time travellers must prevent a catastrophic event that could destroy the fabric of time itself.
9. A group of pirates discover a mysterious island home to a powerful sorceress. They must defeat her and claim her magic for their own before other pirates find out about it.
10. After being banished from their kingdom, a young prince/princess sets out to find a legendary weapon that can restore their honour and reclaim their throne. Along the way, they must confront old enemies and make new allies.

Have a go at "pantsing" a few paragraphs for each idea. If any ideas feel like they have legs then start to plot a more thorough outline and think more deeply about your characters.

Our **Fantasy Writing Workbook** can really help with this stage. You can find it on Amazon now.

Fantasy Writing 101

12

Plotting And Structuring Your Novel

The 3-Act Structure is a popular plotting technique in storytelling, dividing a narrative into three segments: the **setup**, the **confrontation**, and the **resolution**.

- **The setup** introduces the main characters, their environment, and their objectives.
- **The confrontation** brings forth challenges and obstacles that the characters must overcome.
- **The resolution** resolves conflicts and concludes the story in a gratifying manner.

Conflict

Conflict propels the story and creates tension that keeps readers hooked. In a fantasy novel, conflict can be external (e.g., a societal or physical barrier between the main characters) or internal (e.g., personal fears or doubts).

To generate conflict, consider these suggestions:

Analyse your characters: Delve into your characters' desires, goals, fears, and doubts to create conflicts that push them out of their comfort zones.

Utilise external obstacles: External obstacles are beyond the characters' control, like societal or physical barriers. For instance, if your main characters are from different social classes, or tribes, that could create conflict in their relationship. If they live in different countries, or on different planets, that could make being together difficult.

Introduce internal obstacles: Internal obstacles stem from the characters themselves, such as personal fears or doubts. For example, if one of your main characters has been betrayed before and fears being tricked again, that could create conflict in their relationship.

If one character struggles with their identity or self-worth, that could hinder their ability to connect with others.

Generate tension: Keep readers engaged by putting your characters in situations where they must make tough choices or face unexpected challenges. Tension helps maintain reader interest.

Build towards a climax: Escalate the conflict throughout the story, leading to a thrilling climax that keeps readers on edge.

Develop a timeline

After establishing your story idea and characters, create a timeline to organise the plot and track significant events.

To create a timeline:

Begin with major events: Identify the inciting incident, midpoint, and climax, and add them to your timeline.

Fill in the gaps: Include smaller events and conflicts that lead up to the major events in chronological order.

Incorporate character development: Note key moments of character development on your timeline.

Consider pacing: Balance slower, introspective moments with faster-paced action scenes.

Revise as necessary: Update your timeline as your story evolves.

Utilise plot points: These are crucial moments in the story that advance the plot and maintain reader interest. These can include inciting incidents, significant conflicts, and climaxes.

Balance pacing: Ensure your novel's pacing is well-balanced, interweaving action and conflict scenes with slower, more emotional scenes that allow characters to develop and relationships to deepen.

Leverage dialogue: Dialogue is an essential element of any novel. Use dialogue to disclose character traits, build tension, and deepen the relationship between your main characters.

Edit and revise: After completing your first draft, take the time to edit and revise. Address any plot inconsistencies or character development and ensure your story aligns with your original intentions.

Here's an example of what your timeline might look like:

Inciting incident - The protagonist discovers a magical object.

- **Chapters 2-4:** The protagonist sets out on a journey to learn more about the object and the magic in the world.

- **Chapters 5-7:** The protagonist meets other characters and begins to form alliances.

Midpoint - The antagonist is revealed. The stakes are raised.

- **Chapters 9-12:** The protagonist and allies face smaller conflicts and obstacles in preparation for the final battle.
- **Chapters 13-15:** Climax - the final battle takes place.

Resolution - The aftermath of the battle and the protagonist's return home.

13

Creating A Compelling Opening Scene

The opening scene of your fantasy novel is the most important one you will write. You want to grab the reader by the scruff of the neck and refuse to let go of them until the very last line of your novel.

Here are some tips on how to write a brilliant opening scene:

Begin with action: To captivate a reader, open with action. This doesn't have to be a physical action scene, but rather a scene where something occurs that generates tension or conflict.

Introduce your primary characters: Your opening scene is an excellent opportunity to present your main characters, providing readers with an understanding of who they are. Ensure readers have a reason to care about these characters and invest in their journey.

Establish the tone: The opening scene should set the tone for your entire novel. Whether you're writing a lighthearted fantasy romance or a more dramatic novel, the opening should reflect the mood accordingly.

Build suspense: To maintain reader engagement from the beginning, create suspense in the opening scene. This can be achieved by initiating a mystery or presenting a problem that needs resolution.

Employ vivid descriptions: Use vivid descriptions of the setting, characters, and events to captivate the reader and immerse them in your story. Use descriptive language that evokes a vivid image in the reader's mind.

An example incorporating all senses:

The enchanted forest teemed with magic. Upon entering, the sweet scent of blooming flowers filled the air, accompanied by the melodic chirping of birds and the buzzing of insects. The moss-covered ground felt soft underfoot, while beams of sunlight pierced the dense green canopy overhead, casting dappled light on the world below.

Towering and twisted, the trees stood with rough bark. Vines and flowers intertwined around their trunks, forming a vibrant mix of colours and textures. The cool, damp air brushed against the skin, and flutters of wings signalled the fleeting passage of a bird or butterfly.

A realm of wonder and mystery, the forest was a place where anything could transpire. The taste of magic seemed to linger in the air, evoking a sense of excitement and anticipation while exploring its depths.

Commence in the middle: Rather than starting at your story's beginning, consider opening amid the action. This approach can generate urgency and intrigue, making readers eager to learn how the characters arrived at that point.

Establish emotional stakes: Your opening scene should clarify the emotional stakes for your main characters. This can create tension and maintain the reader's interest in the story.

Incorporate dialogue: Dialogue effectively reveals character and generates tension. Consider opening your novel with a conversation between your main characters, hinting at upcoming conflicts.

Maintain brevity: While it's important for your opening scene to be engaging, avoid overwhelming readers with excessive information. Keep your opening scene concise and focused, providing just enough detail to pique the reader's interest and leave them wanting more.

14

Creating Characters

Robust characters are vital for any novel, particularly in a fantasy story. Your characters should be relatable, captivating, and multifaceted. Flesh out their personalities, motivations, and histories to create well-rounded characters that readers can empathise with.

But how do you create captivating characters that readers won't forget?

Establish basic information: Begin by setting up fundamental information about your characters, such as their name, age, gender, occupation, and physical appearance.

Ideas to consider:

Name: Select a name for your character that aligns with the culture and setting of your fantasy world. For instance, in a medieval-inspired world, names like "Aldric" or "Evelynne" might be suitable.

Age: When determining the age of your character, consider the life-span and culture of the world you've created. Characters in a world with magic or supernatural elements may live much longer than humans.

Gender: In a fantasy world, gender roles and expectations might differ from those in the real world. Consider how the gender of your characters impacts their experiences and interactions with others.

Occupation: Reflect on the types of jobs and roles available in your fantasy world. Characters could be warriors, wizards, royalty, or have other distinctive professions fitting the setting.

Physical appearance: Physical appearance may hold greater importance in a fantasy world than in the real world. Consider the various species and races present in your world and their differing appearances. Think about details like skin colour, hair length, and unique features like horns or wings.

Create backgrounds: Develop a backstory for each character that explains their current situation in your story. This can encompass family history, educational background, and career path.

Ideas to consider:

Family history: Reflect on your character's family history and how it influences them. Are they from a lineage of warriors, or are they the first to pursue a magical career? Are their parents alive or deceased?

Educational background: Consider where your character received their education and what they studied. Did they attend an esteemed wizarding school, or were they tutored by a mentor in a less formal setting? Did they struggle with their studies, or were they child prodigies?

Career path: Reflect on your character's career path and how they arrived at their current position in your story. Did they work diligently to earn their place, or did they inherit their role from a family member? Have they encountered any significant challenges or setbacks in their career?

Personal history: Consider any personal experiences that have shaped your character. Have they experienced significant loss, such as the death of a loved one? Have they faced discrimination or prejudice due to their race or background? Have they struggled with addiction or mental illness?

Relationships: Reflect on your character's relationships with others, both past and present. Have they had any significant romantic relationships? Have they maintained close friendships or rivalries? Do they have any siblings or close family members?

Develop personalities: Assign unique personalities to your characters that distinguish them from one another. Using personality tests or character questionnaires may help you develop their traits.

Ideas to consider:

Ambitious and driven: A highly motivated and ambitious character can create conflict and tension in your story. They may be willing to do whatever it takes to accomplish their goals, even if it means sacrificing others along the way.

Empathetic and caring: An empathetic and caring character can evoke empathy and emotional resonance with your readers. A desire to help others and improve the world may be their driving force.

Sarcastic and witty: A sarcastic and witty character can inject humour and lightness into your story. They may use their humour as a defence mechanism or to disarm others.

Mysterious and secretive: A mysterious and secretive character can generate intrigue and suspense in your story. They may have a hidden agenda or past they're trying to conceal.

Rebellious and nonconformist: A rebellious and nonconformist character can challenge the status quo and create conflict in your story. They may desire to break free from societal norms and expectations.

Define goals and motivations: Each character should possess goals and motivations that drive their actions throughout the story. Consider what your characters want and why they want it.

Ideas to consider:

Revenge: Your character may desire revenge against a specific person or group. This could stem from a past betrayal, injustice, or tragedy.

Redemption: Your character may seek redemption for a past mistake or misdeed. They may be driven by a desire to atone for their past actions and gain forgiveness.

Power: A desire for power or control may motivate your character. They may be willing to do whatever it takes to achieve a position of authority or influence.

Love: Your character may be driven by a deep love for another character. They may be willing to risk everything to be with their loved ones or protect them from harm.

Survival: A simple desire to survive may motivate your character into action. They may be facing a life-or-death situation and must do whatever it takes to stay alive.

Discovery: Your character may be driven by a desire to uncover a hidden truth or explore the unknown. They may be motivated by a sense of curiosity and a thirst for knowledge.

Create conflicts: To make your story engaging, create conflicts that challenge your characters and prevent them from achieving their goals. This can include external conflicts, such as a love triangle, or internal conflicts, such as overcoming personal fears or doubts.

Add quirks and flaws: Characters with quirks and flaws are more appealing and relatable to readers. Consider adding quirks or flaws to your characters that make them more unique.

Ideas to consider:

Fear of heights: Your character could have a fear of heights that affects their actions and decisions throughout the story. This could create tension in scenes that take place at high elevations or force the character to find alternative routes to their destination.

Picky eater: Your character could be a picky eater, creating challenges when finding food on their journey. This could also be used to show their personality traits, such as being stubborn or resistant to change.

Perfectionism: Your character could be a perfectionist, creating tension with other more laid-back or improvisational characters. This could also create conflict within the characters as they struggle to balance their desire for perfection with the realities of the situation.

Clumsiness: Your character could be clumsy, causing moments of physical comedy or tension. This could also show vulnerability and create empathy for the character.

Impulsiveness: Your character could be impulsive, which could create moments of unpredictability and tension. This could also be used to show their passion or willingness to take risks.

Build relationships: Relationships between characters are a crucial aspect of any story. Consider how your characters interact with one another and how their relationships evolve throughout the story.

Use foils: Foils are characters with opposing natures that highlight each other's differences. Consider adding a foil character to your story to create more tension and conflict.

Make them dynamic: Dynamic characters change and evolve throughout a story. Consider how your characters grow and change as the story progresses.

Test your characters: Test your characters by placing them in difficult situations and observing their reactions. This can help you better understand their motivations and personalities.

Example:
Suppose you have a character named Aria, who is a skilled warrior. To test her character, you could place her in a situation where she must choose between completing her mission and saving innocent lives.

Aria has been sent on a mission to retrieve a powerful artefact from an enemy stronghold. As she navigates the fortress, she hears cries of pain and desperation coming from a nearby room. Upon investigating, she discovers a group of innocent villagers imprisoned by the enemy.

Aria now faces a difficult choice: continue her mission, leaving the villagers to their fate, or risk everything to save them. Her decision will reveal a lot about her character - is she willing to sacrifice her mission for the greater good? Or is she single-minded in her goal, regardless of the cost to others?

By following these suggestions, you'll create well-rounded, engaging characters that will resonate with your readers.

Create a full character profile - Make your characters come alive!

Do this for each of your main characters:

1. What is the character's name, age, and gender?
2. What is their backstory, and what events in their past have shaped who they are today?
3. What is their personality like? Are they kind and gentle, or harsh and cruel?

4. What are their goals and motivations, and what do they hope to achieve?
5. What are their strengths and weaknesses?
6. What is their occupation or role in the story, and how do they fit into the world you've created?
7. What are their likes and dislikes, and what hobbies or interests do they have?
8. What is their relationship with their family and friends?
9. What is their biggest fear, and what might trigger it?
10. What is their greatest desire, and what lengths would they go to achieve it?
11. What is their moral code, and what lines would they never cross?
12. What is their physical appearance, and how does it reflect their personality?
13. What is their skill set, and what unique abilities or talents do they possess?
14. What is their relationship with magic, and how do they use it (if at all)?
15. What is their social status or class, and how does it affect their interactions with others?
16. What is their romantic history, and what kind of partner are they looking for (if any)?
17. What is their relationship with religion, and what beliefs do they hold?
18. What is their opinion of the other characters in the story?
19. What is their greatest regret, and how does it affect their actions?
20. What are their prejudices or biases, and how do they overcome them (if at all)?
21. What is their sense of humour, and what kind of jokes do they find funny?
22. What are their eating habits and culinary preferences?
23. What is their preferred method of conflict resolution?

24. What is their attitude towards death, and how have they dealt with it in the past?
25. What kind of legacy do they want to leave behind, and how do they want to be remembered?

By the time you have completed this for each of your characters, you will have fully-rounded, believable and engaging characters that will appear in your novel.

15

How To Incorporate Emotions Into Your Fantasy Novel

Emotions are crucial for a successful fantasy novel.

Here are some tips and examples to help you weave emotions into your fantasy novel:

Show, don't tell: Instead of stating a character's feelings, display their emotions through actions, body language, and dialogue. For example, rather than writing, "James was furious," you could depict him clenching his fists, shooting someone a fierce glare, or speaking with a harsh tone.

Use internal monologue: Internal monologue allows readers to peek into a character's thoughts and emotions. Use this technique to reveal how a character feels about a situation or another character.

Example:

Gazing up at the imposing castle walls, Lily felt a surge of apprehension. What if she lacked the strength to fulfil her quest? What if her failure disappointed her allies?

Build tension: Create tension between central characters by introducing conflict and barriers that prevent them from uniting. This tension can evoke a sense of yearning and desire that keeps readers hooked.

Employ sensory details: Use sensory descriptions to paint a vivid picture of the setting and ambiance. This can help readers feel immersed in the story alongside the characters, enhancing the emotional impact.

Example:

Sight: The sun dipped below the horizon, casting elongated shadows on the forest floor. The foliage displayed a vibrant medley of red, orange, and yellow hues, announcing autumn's arrival. As the character ventured further into the woods, they observed beams of light penetrating the canopy, illuminating their path.

Sound: The character heard the wind's melody as it whispered through the trees, causing leaves to rustle and sway. Far off, they discerned the sound of rushing water – perhaps a nearby river. Closer by, they detected the scurrying of tiny creatures in the underbrush, fleeing from the sound of their footsteps.

Smell: The atmosphere was laden with the scent of pine and damp soil – the unmistakable aroma of the forest. The character also detected a faint trace of wood smoke, possibly from a nearby village or camp. A subtle blend of wildflowers and herbs wafted on the breeze, adding a hint of sweetness.

Touch: The character felt the coarse bark of a tree, the grooves and crevices pressing against their fingertips. They grazed their hand against a low branch, appreciating the delicate, velvety texture of the leaves. As they continued, they sensed the ground's unevenness beneath them, with the occasional rock or root threatening to trip them up.

Taste: Pausing to rest, the character sipped from their water flask. The crisp, invigorating water bore an earthy, mineral taste that reminded them of its origin. They retrieved a small piece of hardtack from their pack, the flavour of dry bread and salt filling their mouth.

Vary emotions: Avoid relying solely on a couple of emotions throughout the novel. Mix up the emotions to maintain reader engagement and present a more intricate and authentic portrayal of the characters.

Use dialogue: Dialogue is a potent instrument for exhibiting emotions. Consider how characters converse and how their words convey their emotions.

Create vulnerability: Vulnerability is vital in any narrative. By exposing vulnerability, you enable readers to connect with the characters on a deeper level and become invested in their story.

Employ subtext: Subtext refers to the concealed meaning behind a character's words or actions. Use this method to disclose the characters' genuine emotions and intentions.

Example:

Imagine a scene where Anna confesses her feelings to her love interest, Mark.

Here are some ways to infuse emotions:

- Show Anna's anxiety by having her fiddle with her hands or tap her foot.
- Use internal monologue to reveal Anna's thoughts, such as *"I can't believe I'm doing this. What if he doesn't feel the same way?"*

- Use dialogue to demonstrate Mark's astonishment or bewilderment, such as "I had no idea you felt this way, Anna."
- Incorporate sensory details to create a romantic atmosphere, like flickering candles and gentle music playing in the background.
- Vary the emotions by having Anna experience nervousness, excitement, and vulnerability simultaneously.
- Utilise subtext to reveal that Anna is taking a risk by confessing her feelings, and that Mark's reaction will determine the future of their relationship.

16

Plot Twists

A plot twist is an unexpected turn of events in your story that takes readers by surprise and leaves a lasting impression. It can be a game-changing moment that elevates your narrative and creates a memorable experience for your audience.

A well-executed twist can evoke shock, excitement, and satisfaction, adding depth to characters, altering the story's path, and building suspense.

To craft a successful plot twist, subtly lay the groundwork for the story. The twist should be a logical outcome of previous events while still taking the reader by surprise. You can achieve this through foreshadowing, misdirection, and careful planning.

Here are some plot twist ideas for a fantasy novel:

- The protagonist learns they are not the chosen one but a decoy to distract the real hero.
- The antagonist is the protagonist's long-lost relative with complex motivations.

- The sought-after magical artefact is fake, and the protagonist has unknowingly aided the true villain.
- A trusted mentor or ally secretly works for the enemy, manipulating events from behind the scenes.
- The protagonist's fantastical world is a parallel universe, and they can travel between them.

Three common plot twist types:

The "unreliable narrator" twist: The story's perspective is called into question, creating suspense and adding character layers.

The "red herring" twist: The audience is misled to believe something that is later proven wrong, generating tension.

The "backstory" twist: The audience discovers a character's past that alters their understanding of that character or their actions, adding depth and complexity.

Steps to creating an epic plot twist in a fantasy novel:

Foreshadowing: Prepare readers for the twist by dropping subtle hints, such as mentioning a character's unusual behaviour or having them display ambiguous actions.

Character development: Build believable characters by considering their motives, flaws, and desires. Explore the reasons behind a character's decision to betray their friends, for example.

Misdirection: Keep readers guessing by leading them to believe one thing while setting up a surprise reveal later. Include red herrings or false clues that point towards another character.

Subverting tropes: Twist common fantasy elements to catch readers off guard. Be aware of what readers expect, and then take the trope in an unexpected direction.

Emotional impact: Ensure your plot twist has a meaningful and lasting emotional effect on readers. Consider the consequences of the twist and how it impacts characters and their world.

By following these steps, you'll be able to craft unforgettable plot twists in your fantasy novel, leaving your readers eager for more.

Misconceptions about plot twists

Plot twists are exciting elements in storytelling, but there are several misconceptions surrounding their creation.

Plot twists must be shocking: Plot twists don't have to be a shock to the reader. A great twist should be unexpected and surprising but not necessarily a jaw-dropping moment.

Plot twists come out of the blue: A twist should be unexpected, but not random. Foreshadow the twist and establish its foundation earlier in the story with subtle hints.

All stories need a plot twist: Not every tale requires a twist. Forcing one in where it doesn't belong can feel artificial. Concentrate on telling a captivating story with well-developed characters instead.

The plot twist is the story's most crucial element: While a compelling twist can leave a lasting impression, it's not the only vital part of the story. Characters, themes, and the overall story arc hold equal importance.

Once the twist is revealed, the story ends: A twist should have repercussions that affect the rest of the story. After its revelation, there should be more to tell as characters grapple with the twist's consequences.

Three famous plot twist examples and how you can mirror this in your own writing

The Sixth Sense: This film exemplifies a twist that caught audiences off guard. Believing the protagonist to be a child psychologist aiding a troubled boy, viewers later discover he has been dead the whole time, helping a ghost come to terms with his death.

What you can do in your writing to mirror this plot twist: Use misdirection to lead readers in one direction before surprising them with the truth.

Harry Potter and the Half-Blood Prince: In this book, readers initially perceive Severus Snape as a villain working with the evil Lord Voldemort. At the end, J. K. Rowling reveals Snape as the hero protecting Harry all along.

What you can do in your writing to mirror this plot twist: Use character development to portray a character as a villain, then unveil their true motives and loyalties.

The Empire Strikes Back: This iconic Star Wars film features a shocking twist when Darth Vader reveals he is Luke Skywalker's father. The twist was unforeseen and significantly impacted the story and characters.

What you can do in your writing to mirror this plot twist:
Use foreshadowing to set up the twist while maintaining its unpredictability. Explore the twist's impact on the characters and the story.

17

Red Herrings

Have you ever read a book that kept you guessing until the end? That is thanks to the skill of writing red herrings.

Red herrings are like sneaky baits used by authors to mislead and confuse readers, adding suspense to the narrative and making the big reveal more satisfying.

It's important to know the difference between red herrings and plot twists.

Both are great tools to add complexity and depth to a story, but a red herring is a false sign meant to lead the reader down the wrong pathway in the narrative, while a plot twist is a genuine surprise that changes the direction of the story.

While red herrings can be a fun and effective way to keep readers guessing, it's important to use them wisely. Too many red herrings can be confusing and frustrating for readers, so it's better to use them sparingly and with purpose. Keep your readers on their toes, but do not lead them down too many pointless dark alleys.

Famous red herrings in fantasy novels

The Lord of the Rings: In J. R. R. Tolkien's epic fantasy series, several red herrings keep readers guessing. For example, the character Boromir is set up as a villain beforehand in the story. He's ambitious and aggressive and tries to take the ring from Frodo at one point. It's revealed later that Boromir was floundering with the temptation of the ring and that he eventually sacrifices himself to cover Frodo.

Game of Thrones: In George R. R. Martin's "A Song of Ice and Fire" series, there are several red herrings that keep readers guessing about who the ultimate villain of the story will be. In the series, readers are led to believe that the Lannisters are the main villains, particularly Cersei and Jaime. As the story progresses, it becomes clear there are other forces at work and that the true villain is someone else.

Harry Potter and the Goblet of Fire: In the fourth book in J. K. Rowling's "Harry Potter" series, readers are kept guessing who's responsible for the dark events that are happening in the story. Throughout, readers are led to believe that one of the new characters introduced in the book, particularly Mad-Eye Moody or Barty Crouch Jr., is the culprit. The true villain is revealed at the end to be a completely different character.

How to create red herrings in your fantasy novel

Consider your central riddle or conflict: To produce red herrings, you need to have a central riddle or conflict in your story that you want to mislead readers about. This might be the true identity of the villain, the position of a magical artefact, or the result of a battle.

Develop false leads: Once you've linked your central riddle or conflict, develop false leads that will mislead readers. For example, you might introduce false suggestions or characters that lead the protagonist in the wrong direction if your story is about the hunt for a magical artefact.

Use misdirection: Misdirection is a crucial element in creating effective red herrings. To use misdirection effectively, lead readers in one direction while setting up a surprise reveal later. For example, you might use foreshadowing to make readers believe a particular character is a villain.

Keep it credible. While red herrings are designed to mislead readers, they still need to be believable within the environment of your story. Ensure that your false leads are plausible and do not strain the readers' suspense of disbelief.

Reveal the truth. Make sure that you satisfyingly reveal the truth. The reveal should be surprising, but it should also make sense within the environment of your story.

18

Using Descriptive Language

Using descriptive language is crucial because it contributes to the creation of a vivid and fully realised world for your readers. It enables them to mentally picture the setting, characters, and events. This can make the story seriously captivating and critical.

But be careful not to use too much flowery language because it can make the reader confused and cause them to lose interest in the story. The reader may become overwhelmed and lose track of what's going on if we fill every sentence with detailed descriptions. Using too many adjectives, such as "ethereal" and "diaphanous," for instance, when describing a character might make the reader wonder what the character actually looks like.

Instead, the selective and deliberate use of descriptive language is essential. Make sure that the words you choose add meaning and depth to the story. For instance, instead of describing a character with a lot of adjectives, concentrate on one or two key details that are crucial to the story. For instance, *"Her hair was as dark as midnight, and her eyes sparkled like emeralds."*

Read the two descriptions below. The first paragraph shows how using descriptive language sparingly but effectively can world-build for the reader by offering rich and detailed language to set the scene. The second goes way too overboard with the flowery language and serves to muddy the waters, confusing the reader.

An example of subtle, yet effective, descriptive language:

Wonder and mystery filled the enchanted forest. The branches of the tall, gnarled trees were twisted and turned like serpents. Dappled shadows were cast on the forest floor by the sun's rays as they filtered through the treetops. The sound of rustling leaves and birdsong filled the air, which was thick with the scent of pine and earth.

I could feel the magic pulsing like a living thing around me as I moved deeper into the forest. Maybe every tree, each stone, and each piece of turf was permeated with some old power. I was aware that I was in a significant location and that these woods contained the universe's secrets.

An example of overkill:

A place of wondrous and incomprehensible mystery was the enchanted forest. The tall, gnarled trees were intimidating and formidable, and their gracefully serpentine branches twisted and turned. The forest floor was illuminated by an ethereal and ineffable glow as the sun shone through the lush canopy. The melancholy sound of rustling leaves and sweetly singing birds filled the enchanted atmosphere with a symphony of dulcet melodies, and the heady aroma of fragrant pine and rich, fertile earth filled the air.

I could feel the unchanging magic pulsing around me like a living thing's throbbing, pulsating beat as I walked ever deeper into the forest's heart. It was as if every leaf of grass, every stone, and every tree had an ancient and profound power that resonated with a mysterious energy that I could not comprehend.

Your descriptions must ensure the reader can picture the scene, but don't be tempted to show off your perceived prowess with the English language and go overboard to where your writing is so clogged up with fluff that the descriptions can't shine.

Well-chosen words do the job better than long, convoluted sentences.

19

Writing Dialogue In Your Fantasy Novel

Dialogue is like the beating heart of a story - it's what gives it life and energy, and allows readers to really connect with the characters and the world they inhabit.

Without dialogue, a fantasy novel can feel flat and lifeless, with no real sense of personality or character. But when you add in those juicy conversations, those snappy comebacks, and those heartfelt confessions, things really start to get interesting!

Dialogue allows readers to get to know the characters on a deeper level, to see what makes them tick, what motivates them, and how they interact with one another. It can reveal their fears, their dreams, their quirks, and their flaws.

And let's be real, who doesn't love a good character flaw?

Dialogue isn't just about character development; it also serves a critical role in moving the plot forward. Through conversation, characters can share important information, make plans, and lay out their goals and ambitions. They can argue, scheme, and negotiate, all of which can have huge implications for the story as a whole.

And let's not forget the pure joy of reading well-crafted dialogue - the snappy one-liners, the clever banter, the emotional confessions. It's like a little glimpse into the characters' lives, and it can be so satisfying to watch them interact and grow.

How to show different emotions using dialogue:

Dialogue is a powerful tool when it comes to conveying emotions in a fantasy novel! You see, words have a way of capturing the full range of human experience - from joy and excitement to fear and sorrow, and everything in between. And when those words come from the mouths of your favourite characters, well, it's like an emotional rollercoaster!

Let's start with joy and excitement.

When characters are feeling happy and pumped up, their dialogue can reflect that energy and enthusiasm.

They might use lots of exclamation points, shout out their victories, and revel in their accomplishments.

For example:

"I did it! I actually did it!" exclaimed the young mage, her face lighting up with a huge grin. "I summoned the fire demon!"

Now, on the other end of the spectrum, we have fear and sorrow.

When characters are facing danger or heartache, their dialogue can be much more subdued and tense.

They might speak in hushed tones, struggle to find the right words, or break down into tears.

For example:

"I don't know if we're going to make it out of here alive," whispered the warrior, her voice trembling with fear. *"There are just too many of them."*

And of course, there's anger - one of the most powerful emotions of all. When characters are feeling furious, their dialogue can be downright explosive.

They might shout, insult, or even threaten one another.

For example:

"You think you can just waltz in here and take what's mine?" roared the dragon, flames shooting from his nostrils. *"Think again, little human."*

But emotions aren't always so cut and dry - sometimes they're mixed and complex, like love and longing. When characters are dealing with these feelings, their dialogue can be full of nuance and subtext.

They might flirt, tease, or dance around the subject without ever quite saying what they mean.

For example:

"I know we come from different worlds, and that there are so many things standing in our way," the elven princess said, her eyes locked on the human knight. *"But I can't help the way I feel."*

How you can convey pace using dialogue:

The way characters speak to one another can tell readers a lot about the speed and urgency of a scene. And when it's done right, it can make for one thrilling ride!

For example, when characters are speaking quickly and in a panicked tone, it can convey a sense of urgency and danger.

They might speak in short, clipped sentences, leaving out unnecessary words or details. This can create a sense of tension and excitement, as readers feel like they're right in the middle of the action.

For example:

"Run! They're coming!" yelled the young hero, his heart pounding in his chest. "We have to get out of here, now!"

On the other hand, when characters speak more slowly and deliberately, it can convey a sense of calm or even tension.

They might take their time, carefully choosing their words or pausing for effect. This can create a sense of anticipation, as readers wait for the next shoe to drop.

For example:

"I have something to tell you," the wizard said, his voice low and measured. "Something that might change everything."

And let's not forget about silence. Sometimes, the absence of dialogue can be just as powerful as the words themselves.

A scene with no dialogue at all can create a sense of stillness or calm, while a scene with lots of interruptions or overlapping speech can convey a sense of chaos or conflict.

For example:

Fantasy Writing 101

The battle raged on, with swords clashing and magic crackling through the air. The heroes fought with all their might, but it seemed like the enemy was endless. They spoke not a word, each lost in their own thoughts and fears.

So you see, dialogue in a fantasy novel can do so much more than just convey information - it can also convey a sense of pace and urgency, bringing the story to life in a way that's thrilling and engaging.

20

How To End Your Novel

Good endings are absolutely crucial when it comes to writing a successful fantasy novel. And if we're being honest with ourselves, the ending is usually the scene we cannot get out of our heads before we even start writing. It rattles around in the brain, and you cannot stop thinking about how cool it would be if 'xyz…' happened. The content of the novel is just all the scenes that lead up to this epic, blockbuster ending.

The ending is the last thing your readers will experience, and it's what will stay with them long after they've finished the book. If your ending isn't up to scratch, it can leave a bad taste in their mouth and prevent them from recommending your book to others.

A good ending is essential because it provides closure for the reader and resolves any questions or conflicts from the story. It's the ultimate payoff for everything that's come before, and it can leave readers feeling satisfied, moved, or even changed.

A strong ending can also help solidify your reputation as a writer, building your brand and attracting new readers to your work.

Fantasy Writing 101

But what happens if your ending isn't good?

Unfortunately, it can have some serious consequences for your writing business. Readers may leave negative reviews or give up on your work altogether, hurting your sales and damaging your reputation. You may also struggle to get your work published in the future, as editors and agents will be hesitant to take on a writer with a track record of weak endings.

There are so many ways to wrap up a story, each with its own unique twists and turns. Let's explore some of the many ways you could end your fantasy novel - some of which might just surprise you!

The happy ending: This is the classic way to end a story, with all loose ends tied up and the heroes riding off into the sunset. Think "The Lord of the Rings" or "Harry Potter and the Deathly Hallows."

How to do it:

- Ensure that all loose ends are tied up, so readers feel a sense of closure.
- Give readers a satisfying payoff for the challenges the characters have faced.
- End on a note of hope and optimism, so readers feel uplifted and inspired.

The bittersweet ending: This is a more complex and nuanced way to end a story, where the heroes may have achieved their goals but at a cost. Think "The Hunger Games" or "The Dark Knight Rises."

How to do it:

- Make sure the ending feels earned and in line with the story's themes.
- Use the ending to highlight the costs and sacrifices that the characters have made.
- Give readers a sense of emotional complexity, with both joy and sadness coexisting.

The open-ended ending: This is where you leave some things unresolved, allowing readers to speculate and imagine what might happen next. Think "Inception" or "The Giver."

How to do it:

- Decide which questions to leave unanswered and which threads to tie up.
- Provide enough information for readers to draw their own conclusions.

Make sure the ending feels intentional and not a cop-out.

The twist ending: This is where you pull the rug out from under your readers, revealing a shocking surprise at the end. Think "The Sixth Sense" or "Fight Club."

How to do it:

- Plant clues throughout the story that will lead readers to the twist, but make them subtle enough that readers won't catch on too early.
- Make sure the twist is earned and doesn't feel like a cheap trick.

- Ensure that the twist is satisfying and doesn't leave readers feeling cheated.

The tragic ending: This is where everything falls apart and the heroes are left with nothing. Think "Romeo and Juliet" or "Game of Thrones" (book version).

How to do it:

- Make sure the ending feels earned and is in line with the story's themes.
- Give readers a sense of catharsis, even if it's a painful one.
- Use the ending to make a powerful statement about the human condition.

The ambiguous ending: This is where you leave things deliberately unclear, allowing readers to draw their own conclusions. Think "Blade Runner" or "No Country for Old Men."

How to do it:

- Decide which questions to leave unanswered and which threads to tie up.
- Use the ending to encourage readers to think critically about the story's themes and messages.
- Make sure the ending feels intentional and not a cop-out.

The epilogue: This is where you show what happens to the characters after the main events of the story have concluded. Think "The Return of the King" or "The Last Battle."

How to do it:

- Use the epilogue to tie up any loose ends that couldn't be addressed in the main story.
- Give readers a sense of closure and resolution.
- Use the epilogue to hint at the characters' future without revealing too much.

The flashback ending: This is where you reveal a key piece of information that changes everything. Think "The Usual Suspects" or "The Prestige."

How to do it:

- Use the flashback to reveal something that changes the reader's understanding of the story.
- Make sure the revelation feels earned and isn't too obvious.
- Use the flashback to deepen the themes and messages of the story.

The meta ending: This is where you break the fourth wall and reveal that the story is just a story. Think "Stranger Than Fiction" or "The NeverEnding Story."

How to do it:

- Use the ending to comment on the nature of storytelling itself.

- Make sure the ending feels earned and isn't too gimmicky.
- Use the ending to make a statement about the role of stories in our lives.

The 'choose-your-own-ending' ending: This is where you give readers multiple options for how the story could end, allowing them to choose their own adventure. Think "Bandersnatch" or "The Stanley Parable."

How to do it:

- Use the ending to give readers agency and a sense of ownership over the story.
- Make sure the different endings are distinct and meaningful.
- Use the endings to highlight different aspects of the story's themes and messages.

How to arrive at the ending you want

Ensuring that you arrive at the ending you want in your fantasy novel can be a challenging task, but with the right plotting techniques, it's definitely possible!

Here are a few tips to help you get there:

Start with the ending in mind: Before you begin writing your novel, make sure you have a clear idea of how you want it to end. This will help you plot out the story in a way that builds towards that ending.

Create a detailed outline: Once you know how your story will end, create a detailed outline that breaks down each chapter and scene. This will help you stay on track and ensure that each part of the story is leading towards the ending you want.

Use the three-act structure: The three-act structure (beginning, middle, and end). Make sure that each act has a clear goal and conflict, and that each scene moves the story forward.

Use foreshadowing: By dropping hints about the ending throughout the story, you can create a sense of inevitability and make the ending feel earned.

Revise and refine: As you write, be open to making changes to your outline and story to ensure that you're heading towards the ending you want. This may mean cutting scenes that aren't working or adding new ones that build towards the ending.

Get feedback: Once you've finished your draft, get feedback from beta readers or writing groups. This can help you identify areas where the story isn't working and make changes to ensure that you're heading towards the ending you want.

With a little planning and hard work, you can create a story that builds towards a satisfying and powerful conclusion.

21

Fantasy Novel Book Titles

An engaging title captures readers' attention and keeps them invested in the story.

An effective step for beginners would be to brainstorm several title ideas before asking friends or beta readers which one they find most captivating.

Include elements of the story in your title: Incorporating elements of your story into your title gives readers a taste of what to expect from your novel. Examples of famous fantasy novel titles that do this are "The Chronicles of Narnia" by C. S. Lewis, "The Name of the Wind" by Patrick Rothfuss, and "The Wheel of Time" by Robert Jordan.

An effective step for beginners would be identifying key components of their plot line and brainstorming title options that incorporate them.

Be unique: Being original is essential in the fantasy genre. Examples of notable novel titles that stand out include "The Once and

Future King" by T. H. White, "The Lies of Locke Lamora" by Scott Lynch, and "The Hundred Thousand Kingdoms" by N. K. Jemisin.

A great starting point for new fantasy novelists would be researching other titles in the genre and then brainstorming several unique and original ideas.

Keep it short and memorable: Short, catchy titles are easier for readers to remember and can better engage their attention. Examples of famous fantasy novel titles that follow this rule include "The Hobbit" by J. R. R. Tolkien, "Eragon" by Christopher Paolini, and "Mistborn" by Brandon Sanderson.

As a beginner, try keeping titles short but sweet; avoid long or convoluted ones that could be difficult to recall later on.

22

Fantasy Writing Word Count

Word count in fantasy writing isn't a set formula. Fantasy novels can range in length from short novellas to epic series that span thousands of pages; however, as a general guideline, most fantasy novels fall somewhere between **80,000-150,000 words.**

As a new fantasy fiction writer, it's essential to remember that while word count matters, it isn't the most critical aspect of your story. What matters more is crafting an intriguing and captivating tale that connects with readers.

Here are a few tips to ensure your story stays on track:

Plan your story: Before you begin writing, take time to plan out your story. This could involve creating an outline, developing characters, and selecting key plot points. Doing this helps keep you focused and prevents you from deviating from the intended path. Our workbook, **"How to Write a Winning Fiction Book Outline – Fantasy Fiction Workbook,"** will help you do this perfectly.

Focus on the main plot: Subplots can add depth to your story, but you must stay focused on the main one. Doing so helps avoid unnecessary detours and keeps your narrative moving forward.

Keep the pacing in mind: A successful fantasy novel should maintain a steady pace that keeps readers interested. Be mindful of this aspect and avoid lingering on any one scene or detail for too long.

Edit and revise: Once your first draft is complete, take time to edit and revise it. Doing this will help cut out any unnecessary dithering and guarantee your story stays on track.

Remember, writing a fantasy novel is an adventure, and it's essential to focus on the story first and foremost. Word count may be important, but it should never be your sole measure of success. Keep writing; stay committed to your project, and with time and practice, you'll develop your own distinct voice and style.

23

Fantasy Fiction Book Cover Tips

They say you should never judge a book by its cover. Well, unfortunately, we all do this. A good book cover is one of the most important ways to attract readers, so it must encapsulate the theme and tone of the book.

Fantasy fiction book covers often feature imagery associated with the genre, such as:

Magical elements: Fantasy novels often incorporate magical elements such as spells, potions and enchanted objects into their storylines. Book covers may feature imagery reflecting these elements, such as wands, crystal balls, or creatures from mystical realms.

Mythical creatures: Many fantasy novels feature mythical creatures such as dragons, unicorns and griffins on book covers - either as the main focus or background element.

Landscapes: Fantasy novels often take place in fantastical worlds with striking landscapes. Book covers may feature imagery that captures these worlds, such as mountains, forests, or castles.

Heroes: Many fantasy novels showcase heroic characters on epic quests. Book covers may show these heroes in action, wielding weapons or engaging in battle.

Dark elements: Some fantasy novels contain darker themes or include villains and dark magic. Book covers may feature imagery to reflect these elements, such as skulls, dark forests, or ominous symbols.

What you can do:

Research other book covers: Take a look at other fantasy book covers to gain an idea of what works and doesn't. Be mindful of typography, colour schemes, and imagery when choosing your design elements.

Choose a theme: Select an aesthetic for your book cover that accurately reflects the genre and tone of your story. For instance, if it's dark and moody, use darker colours and imagery to convey this mood.

Keep it simple: A busy book cover can be disorienting and overwhelming. Keep your design minimal, with only one or two key elements that stand out.

Use high-quality images: Select high-quality images that are pertinent to your story and visually pleasing. Steer clear of low-quality or blurry photographs.

Be mindful of typography: Select a font that is legible and suitable for your story. Avoid using too many different fonts or styles on one cover; this can create an unorganised visual.

Consider the format: When designing your book cover, take into account the format. If it's an ebook, opt for a simpler design that looks good at smaller sizes.

Request feedback: Seek feedback from others on your book cover design in order to identify areas for improvement and ensure that it resonates with potential readers.

Remember, your book cover is the first thing potential readers will see, so make it stand out and be captivating. With these tips and practical strategies, you can design an effective fantasy fiction book cover that will draw readers to your story.

24

Editors And Proofreaders

Editors and proofreaders are incredibly important in the 'page-to-published' process for authors. They help to develop a weak storyline, weed out boring, redundant characters, and sharpen up dialogue throughout your novel. But firstly, how do you know which type of editor you need?

Here are different types of editors and a breakdown of what they do:

Developmental editor: A developmental editor reviews a manuscript's structure and content for structural errors or weaknesses. They assist authors in crafting storylines, characters, and themes, as well as providing constructive criticism on areas that need improvement.

Developmental editors are essential in helping authors craft an organised and compelling narrative.

Copy editor: A copy editor oversees the technical aspects of a manuscript, such as grammar, punctuation, spelling and syntax.

They guarantee that the text is free from errors and consistent in style and tone.

Ultimately, copy editors are essential in producing an elegant and professional final product.

Line editor: Line editors focus on the individual sentences and paragraphs of a manuscript, making sure the language is crystal clear, concise, and captivating. They may suggest rewording sentences, cutting unnecessary words, or adding descriptive language to strengthen the story.

Line editors are essential in producing polished writing that works effectively.

Proofreader: Proofreaders are responsible for catching any remaining mistakes or typos in a manuscript before it's published. They review the final copy and guarantee it's free of mistakes, providing you with an error-free final product.

Editors and proofreaders are essential for producing a high-quality final product. They offer invaluable feedback and suggestions to help authors craft captivating manuscripts.

When searching for an editor and proofreader, it's essential to consider their experience, rates, and areas of specialisation. Freelance marketplaces and traditional publishing houses both provide excellent opportunities to find an editor who meets your requirements.

25

Book Marketing

Marketing your book correctly can mean the difference between failing to sell a single copy, and becoming a bestseller in your niche. Get it right, and the world will know your name.

Here are some book marketing tips to help you succeed with your fantasy book:

Create a website: Sign up for either WordPress or Wix's free accounts, choose a template, and customise it with your book's information and images.

Create an email list: Utilise Mailchimp or ConvertKit to create a landing page, offering readers free samples of chapters or short stories in exchange for their email addresses. Promote this landing page via social media channels and online communities.

Utilise social media: Establish a Facebook, Twitter and Instagram profile and post regular updates about your writing process. Include relevant hashtags in your posts to reach a wider, but specific to your niche, audience.

Guest blog: Research blogs and websites related to your genre, identify the contact information for their owners or editors, and propose a guest post idea.

An example email to help you with the above tip:

Subject: Guest Post Proposal

Dear [Owner/Editor's Name],

Hope this email finds you well. My name is [Your Name], and I am a fantasy fiction author. After discovering your blog/website [Blog/Website Name], I was greatly inspired by the information you offer your readers. I look forward to continuing our correspondence!

As a fan of fantasy fiction, I would like to suggest a guest post topic that may be of interest to your readers. The post would be about [Detail your proposed topic and its relationship to the blog/website content].

I have attached an outline of the post for your review. Let me know if this is something you would be interested in sharing with your audience, and I will happily make any necessary modifications to fit within your blog/website's style and tone.

Thank you for considering my proposal and I look forward to hearing from you shortly.

Best Regards,
[Your Name]

Participate in online communities: Search out forums, groups and communities related to your niche and join them. Participate in discussions while sharing updates about your book with them. Be mindful though not to spam or self-promote excessively.

Offer free copies: Reach out to book bloggers, reviewers and readers through email or social media and offer them complimentary copies of your book in exchange for honest reviews.

Some writers find this a hard thing to do, to give away freebies after all the hard work and cost they might have gone to to get their book in print. But sometimes you have to speculate to accumulate, as they say, and giving away a free copy of your book will introduce you to your target audience, who then may pay money for your next book if they like your writing.

If you are really set against giving your whole novel away for free then consider writing an additional short story or novella and presenting it for free to book bloggers as a "lead magnet" to your writing portfolio. By doing this, they can get to know your writing style and then potentially recommend your full-length novel to their audience.

Example email to help you:

Subject: Free Copy for Honest Review

Dear [Name of Reviewer/Blogger/Reader],

Hope this email finds you well. My name is [Your Name], and I am a fantasy fiction author. After discovering your book review/blog on [Blog/Website Name], I was highly impressed with your work.

As someone who enjoys reading and reviewing fantasy novels, I would like to offer you a complimentary copy of [Book Title] in exchange for an honest review on your blog/Amazon/Goodreads account.

I believe my book would be of interest to you and your readers and would love to hear your opinion. If so, please reach out and I will send you a free copy in any format desired.

Thank you for taking the time to talk with me today; I look forward to hearing from you shortly.

Best regards,
[Your Name]

Run a giveaway: Use social media to host an online giveaway of your book or related merchandise. Encourage readers to spread the news of this opportunity to earn additional entries for sharing with their friends.

Attend book events: Research local book events and attend them with copies of your book to sell or give away. Be friendly and approachable when speaking to potential readers.

Collaborate with other authors: Reach out to other authors in your genre via social media or email and offer to cross-promote each other's books.

Use book promotion sites: Research book promotion sites like BookBub, BookGorilla and Bargain Booksy and apply for free or low-cost options.

Request reviews: Reach out to friends, family and colleagues via email or social media and invite them to leave reviews on Amazon and Goodreads. Don't incentivise or pressure them into leaving positive reviews; rather, simply ask for their opinion.

Create a book trailer: Use free video editing software such as iMovie or Windows Movie Maker to craft an engaging book trailer with images, music, and text. Share the trailer on social media channels and your website for maximum exposure.

Utilise local media: Explore local newspapers, radio stations and TV stations and reach out to see if they would be interested in featuring or interviewing you for your book. Have a polished pitch ready.

An example email to help you:

Subject: Request for Book Review, Feature or Interview

Dear [Name of Contact Person],

Hello, my name is [Your Name], and I am a fantasy fiction author. I am reaching out to you because I think your readers/listeners/viewers would be interested in hearing about my new book, [Book Title].

[Contain a brief overview of your book, such as its genre and an outline with one or two sentences about the plot.]

I'm thrilled to share my book with the local community and was wondering if you would be interested in featuring it in your publication/show? Alternatively, I would be delighted to participate in an interview where we can discuss my book and its creation process.

I have attached a press release and author bio for your reference, as well as a complimentary copy of my book in case you would like to review it prior to the feature or interview. I would be more than happy to provide any additional information or answer any queries you may have.

Thank you for taking the time to respond. I look forward to hearing from you shortly.

Best wishes,
[Your Name]

Utilise Amazon author pages: Create an Amazon author page and fill it with your book's details, images, and bio. Use the page to promote your book and connect with readers.

Connect with book clubs: Research book clubs in your area or online and reach out to organisers to join discussions about your book. Be respectful and accepting of different opinions.

26

Fantasy Writing Glossary

A - Arcane: Refers to anything relating to magic or the supernatural.

B - Bestiary: A collection of mythical or imaginary creatures.

C - Chosen One: A common fantasy trope in which a character is chosen by fate or prophecy to save the world.

D - Dragon: A large, mythical fire-breathing reptile.

E - Enchantment: The use of magic to create a spell or charm.

F - Fantasy: A genre of fiction that often includes elements of magic, the supernatural, or otherworldly creatures.

G - Goblin: A small, mischievous creature often found in fantasy stories.

H - Hero's Journey: A narrative structure that is commonly used in fantasy fiction, in which the hero goes on a journey of self-discovery and personal growth.

I - Incantation: A spoken or written spell or charm.

J - Jousting: A medieval sport in which knights on horseback engage in combat.

K - Knight: A noble warrior, often associated with medieval times.

L - Lore: The collective knowledge, myths, and legends of a particular world or culture.

M - Magic: The use of supernatural powers to create a desired effect.

N - Necromancy: The use of magic to communicate with or control the dead.

O - Ogre: A large, fearsome creature often depicted as having a monstrous appearance.

P - Prophecy: A prediction or foretelling of future events, often found in fantasy stories.

Q - Quest: A journey or mission undertaken by a character to achieve a goal.

R - Royalty: A ruling class, often associated with medieval times and fantasy fiction.

S - Sorcery: The use of magic to manipulate or control the natural world.

T - Troll: A large and brutish mythical creature often found in fantasy stories.

U - Unicorn: A mythical creature, typically depicted as a horse with a single horn on its forehead.

V - Vampire: A mythical, undead creature that feeds on the blood of the living.

W - Wizard: A powerful magic user, often associated with fantasy stories and mythology.

X - Xenophobia: The fear or dislike of foreign or unfamiliar people, often found in fantasy stories as a theme or plot point.

Y - Yeti: A mythical creature typically depicted as large and ape-like.

Z - Zombie: An undead creature often found in fantasy stories, usually shown as a reanimated corpse.

Now what...?

Now that you're equipped with the knowledge and tools to write your very own page-turning fantasy novel, it's time to take action and make it happen!

Our **"How To Write A Winning Fiction Book Outline -**

Now what...?

Fantasy Fiction Workbook" provides all the resources and guidance you need to bring your book to life with ease and enjoyment.

With our done-for-you novel outline templates and prompts, you can create a captivating story from scratch. We'll guide you through every step of the process, from planning and writing, to publishing and beyond.

Imagine holding your book in your hands, knowing that readers are eagerly waiting to devour your story. With our winning strategy and your unique ideas, success is within reach.

And the best part? You can make money while you sleep, as your book reaches readers around the world.

Our workbook is the tool you wished you had from the beginning, providing all the resources and guidance you need to turn your ink into income. So what are you waiting for?

Grab your copy of **"How to Write a Winning Fiction Book Outline - Fantasy Fiction Workbook"** now and let us help you take your writing to the next level.

Your readers are waiting for your amazing story, and we're here to help you make it happen – every step of the way.

Vicky & Claire

HackneyandJones.com

www.ingramcontent.com/pod-product-compliance
Lightning Source LLC
Chambersburg PA
CBHW050301120526
44590CB00016B/2446